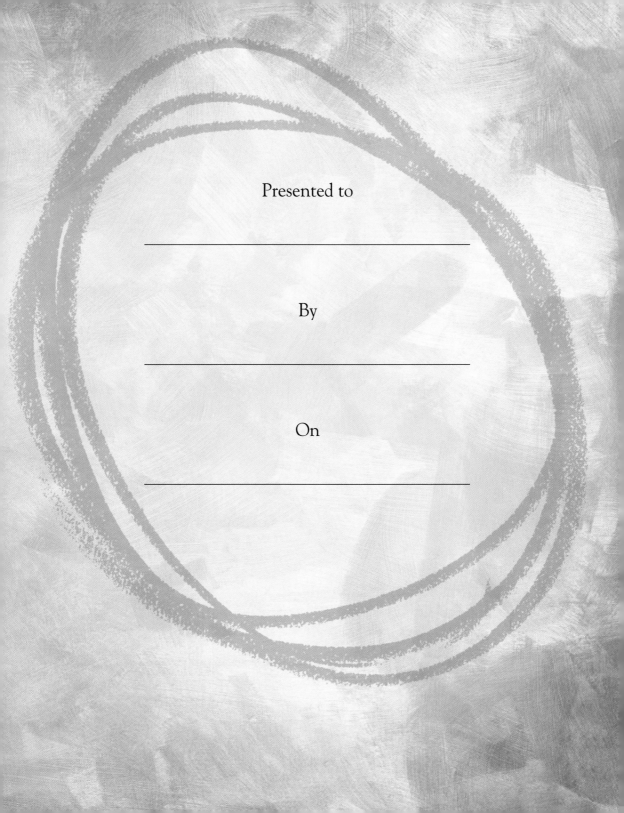

Presented to

_____

By

_____

On

_____

Big Dreams & Powerful Prayers

Illustrated Bible

Mark Batterson

with Glenys Nellist

Illustrated by Omar Aranda

ZONDERKIDZ

Big Dreams and Powerful Prayers Illustrated Bible
Copyright © 2019 by Mark Batterson
Illustrations © 2019 by Omar Aranda

Requests for information should be addressed to:
Zonderkidz, 3900 Sparks Drive, Grand Rapids, Michigan 49546

Hardcover ISBN: 978-0310-74682-9
Ebook ISBN: 978-0310-74691-1

Art direction and design: Kris Nelson/StoryLook Design

Printed in China

19 20 21 22 23 24 25 26 27 28 / LPC / 10 9 8 7 6 5 4 3 2 1

To my mom and dad,
Some of my earliest memories are the Bible stories you read at bedtime.
Those stories sunk into my subconscious, becoming the seedbed of big dreams
and powerful prayers. May this book do for others what those stories did for me.
–MB

Dedicated to my mother.
–OA

Dear Reader,

Some of my earliest memories are the Bible storybooks my parents read to me as child. Some of those stories stamped my imagination, helping me dream God-sized dreams. Other stories sunk into my subconscious, time capsules of God's grace, God's goodness. Either way, those Bible stories forever shaped the way I think, the way I live.

I have a theory: *over time, our favorite verses of Scripture become the script of our lives.* As we live out the promises of God, those verses become the storylines of our lives. And our lives become a subplot in the story God has been writing throughout history.

One of those subplots is a little-known story about Honi, a man who became known as "the circle maker" because of a bold prayer he prayed. Inspired by the prophets who had gone before him, Honi exercised Elijah-like faith when a drought threatened to destroy his people.

Honi made a circle in the parched sand and vowed that he would not leave that circle until it rained. Although he was an old man, Honi's childlike faith and complete reliance on God's promises saved a generation of Jews, the generation before Jesus.

My prayer for every child who reads these stories is a revelation that they, like the characters of the Bible and like the Honis of this world, play a unique role in the story of God. Jesus is the "author" of our faith, and if we give him complete editorial control over our lives, he writes amazing stories through us.

My prayer for every parent is that you'll "become like little children" once again. May the stories remind you of God's faithfulness as they stretch your faith!

Blessings,

Mark Batterson

Old Testament

New Testament

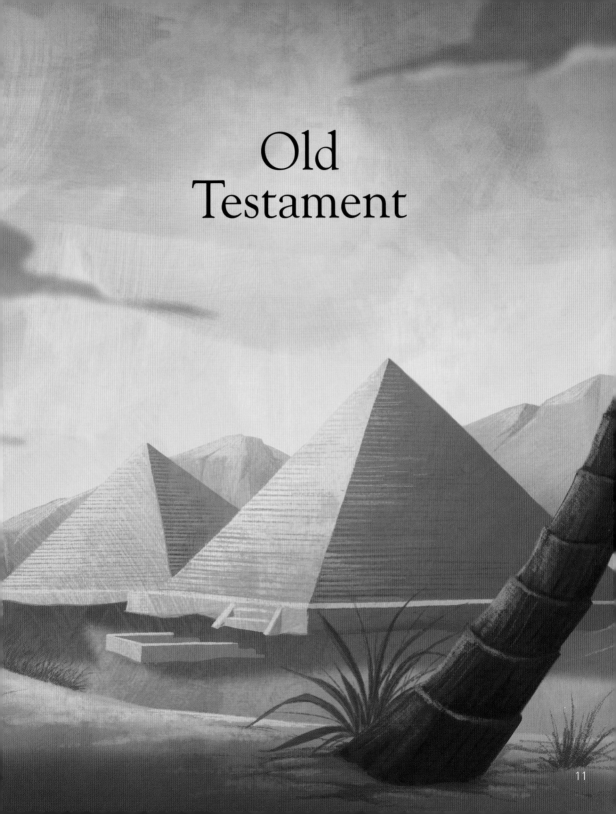

Old Testament

In the Beginning

GENESIS 1–2

In the beginning, there was nothing to see—no earth spinning in space, no shining sun, no twinkling stars, no peeping moon. There was only darkness. But in the darkness, something was moving. You couldn't see it and you couldn't hear it, but it was there. God's spirit was hovering, getting ready to create the world.

Into the darkness, God spoke. He only said four little words. But those four little words had the power to create something from nothing:

"Let there be light."

And then came the miracle. At the sound of God's voice, the darkness flew away. A brilliant light danced and swirled as it filled the space with warmth.

As God's handiwork continued, mountains rose from the deep to touch the skies, oceans swelled and roared, and the rivers laughed as they ran. God clapped his hands in delight—it was so good!

Birds flew high on the wing in this wonderful world that God had made. Creatures crawled and hopped and slithered on the land; fishes dived in the deep. The earth was filled with the colors and sounds and movements of life.

In the garden of Eden, fantastic fruit hung from the trees; grass grew tall and green; flowers nodded in the wind and filled the air with perfume. After five busy days, God had everything in place. The world was ready for his children.

God bent down, scooped the dust up into his hands, and
breathed life into Adam; then, while Adam slept, he created Eve.
"Look," he said, when each of his children opened their eyes. "I am
giving all of this to you."

Adam and Eve ran barefoot through the garden, holding hands and laughing. Each day, they would come and talk to God. And the creator of the world watched over them with pride. They were his, they were blessed, and they were good.

There Is Power in Prayer!

Ever since God created Adam and Eve, he has wanted to talk with his children. The creator of the universe wants to talk with you too! Nothing makes God smile more than when he hears you talking and praying to him. And there is so much to learn about prayer by reading the Bible. From the first page to the last, the Bible is filled with stories about people who talked with God, listened to his voice, and learned the power of prayer. Whether their prayers were whispered behind closed doors or shouted in the streets; whether they prayed out loud or in silence; whether their prayer was a cry for help or a song of praise, all these people discovered the same wonderful truth—God hears every prayer and answers every cry. The same God who hovered over the world at the beginning of creation is hovering over your life too—watching over you, ready to talk with you and show you how powerful prayers can be. Are you ready?

Dear God,
It's such an awesome feeling to know that you,
the creator of the universe, want to talk with me!
Be with me as I read this book. Help me to listen to your words
through its pages and learn more about the power of prayer.
Amen.

Know that the Lord is God. He made us, and we belong to him.

PSALM 100:3

In the Garden

GENESIS 3

It was sunrise in the garden of Eden. Eve was out for an early morning stroll. The sun rose high in the sky and its rays sparkled on the fruit that hung from the tree in the middle of the garden. It looked so good! What a shame that God had told her and Adam not to eat it.

"It tastes as delicious as it looks, you know," a sneaky voice said. Eve turned to see a big snake coiled around a nearby tree.

"I'm sure it does," replied Eve. "But Adam and I can't eat that. God told us not to. If we even touch it, we will die."

"Nonsense!" the naughty snake hissed. "You won't die. If you eat the fruit, you will be like God."

Eve reached out and plucked the delicious fruit from the tree. She turned it over in her hand, smelled it, brought it to her mouth, and took one small bite.

Then she gave some to Adam. Instantly, they knew something was wrong. The sun seemed to disappear behind the clouds. Dark shadows stretched across the garden. Adam and Eve felt cold. Why did they eat that fruit? How could they talk to God now? They slipped behind a tree and waited.

"Where are you?" God's voice rang out clear and crisp in the cool of the evening. His words echoed above the moonlit trees as he walked quietly through the garden. God was looking for his children.

But Adam and Eve stayed where they were. They knew they should never have eaten that fruit. Adam was afraid, but he knew he had to talk to God. And so, gathering up courage, he held Eve's hand and stepped out from behind the tree.

"We're here, God," said Adam. "We heard you calling. But we were scared."

"Did you eat the fruit I told you not to?" God's voice trembled and his heart filled with sadness as Adam and Eve looked up at him. What would happen now? Would God stop loving them? NO! That would never happen!

God could never take his love away. Adam and Eve were more precious to him than jewels. They were the ones God made the whole world for; the ones he painted the sky for; the ones he grew the garden for; the ones he created with his very own breath.

God bent down, gently picked up his children, and covered them in warm clothes. Before they had to leave the garden forever because of their sin, he whispered softly, "I'll never stop loving you."

The gates to the garden of Eden were closed. Adam and Eve could never find their way back there. But the way to God's heart was open. They could always find their way back to him.

Prayer Is Always the Way Back to God

Did you know that prayer is always the way back to God? Whenever you do something you know isn't right, tell God. Never be afraid to talk to him. God is waiting to hear from you—when you've done something wrong; when you've done something right; in happy times and in sad times. And it's when you talk to God that you discover just how wonderful he really is. God is a great big God who not only forgives, he loves to keep his promises, answer prayers, work miracles, and make his dreams for your life come true. Talk to God—he is ready and waiting.

Dear God,
Thank you that I can talk to you
about anything, anytime, anywhere.
Amen.

You will come and pray to me.
And I will listen to you.

JEREMIAH 29:12

In the Rain

GENESIS 6:8—8:22

Noah scratched his beard. He looked down at his toolbox and couldn't help but wonder, had God *really* told him to build a big boat? Noah had never been sailing in his life. There were no lakes or oceans nearby. But Noah *knew* God. He talked to God every day. And if God told him to build that huge boat, he would do it, no matter how silly it seemed.

Noah got straight to work. Every day and every night, the sounds of sawing wood and hammering nails echoed above the hills and the valleys around Noah's home. Noah carefully followed every single one of God's directions, until finally, one day, his huge and wonderful boat was finished.

"We're ready, dear," Noah shouted to his wife.

"Ready for what?" she replied.

"Ready to fill the ark with animals!" said Noah with a grin. "We must make room for two of every kind of animal and help them into the ark. God is going to send a mighty flood over the earth to clean it. But don't worry. We'll be safe inside."

So Noah, his wife, and his family got to work. Into the ark the animals trotted, crawled, flew, and slithered; until one day, the heavens opened and the rain came falling down.

God closed the door of the ark as the mighty waters rose and covered the whole earth. For forty long days and forty long nights, the rains fell down. Inside the ark, Noah waited, and waited, and waited. Noah knew that God would keep his promise. He knew that he and his family would be safe.

And then, one day, the rain stopped. God opened the door of the ark and everyone came out to a new, clean earth. All the animals disappeared into the woods and the fields, ready to build a new home for themselves. But the first thing Noah built was not a house. Noah built an altar to God, where he made a burned sacrifice to God. And high in the sky, above Noah's head, God flung a huge, shining rainbow. "I'll never flood the earth again," God whispered. And Noah, who *always* listened to God, smiled.

Obey God, Even if It Seems Silly

If someone asked you what prayer was all about, what would you say? Would you tell them that prayer is a time when we talk to God? It is. But prayer is also a time when God talks to *us*. So it's very important that we listen. What do you think might have happened if Noah hadn't listened to God and followed his directions? Suppose he hadn't built that boat because it seemed like a silly thing to do? But Noah listened and obeyed. As you pray, try to listen, wait, trust, and follow God's direction, *even* if it seems silly.

Dear God,
When I spend time with you,
help me not to do all the talking.
Help me to listen, deep in my heart,
for what you might whisper to me.
Then help me to obey.
Amen.

**Blessed are those who hear
God's word and obey it.**

LUKE 11:28

Under the Stars

GENESIS 15:1–6

Abram was one of God's finest friends. He talked to God every day, listened to God, and followed all his instructions. Abram trusted God enough to leave his home behind and trudge through deserts, fields, and forests to find the new home that God had for him. But now that his travels were done, Abram felt sad. What did the future hold? God still hadn't given him the very thing he wanted—a son.

It was Abram and his wife Sarai's dream to have a little boy. Surely one baby boy was not too much to ask. But they still were not parents, and Abram didn't know why.

"Don't be afraid, Abram," said God. "I'm like a strong shield around you; I'm your great prize."

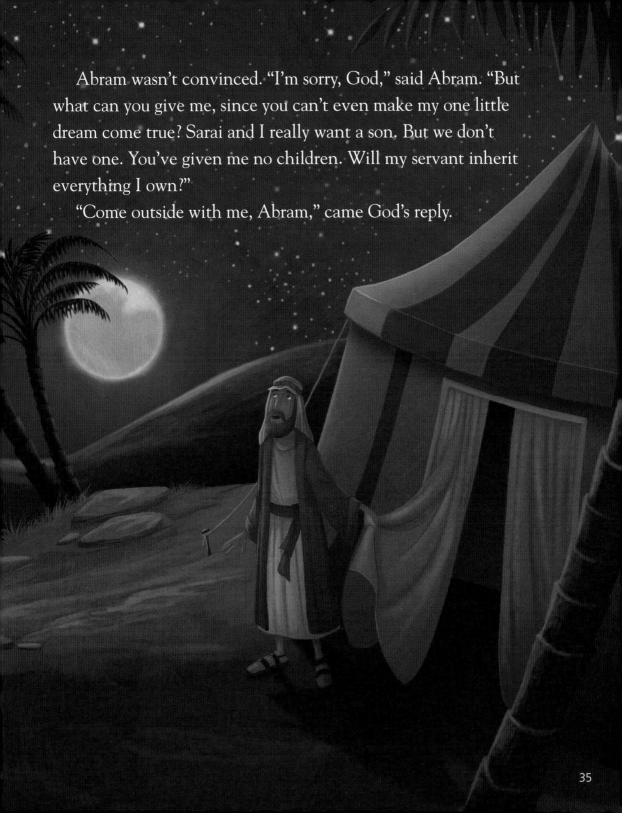

Abram wasn't convinced. "I'm sorry, God," said Abram. "But what can you give me, since you can't even make my one little dream come true? Sarai and I really want a son. But we don't have one. You've given me no children. Will my servant inherit everything I own?"

"Come outside with me, Abram," came God's reply.

It was dark outside. The night sky was alive with a million twinkling stars that danced above Abram's head. "Can you count those stars, Abram?" asked God.

"Of course not!" laughed Abram. It was impossible. No one could count so many! "Well, guess what?" said God, with a twinkle in his eye. "You won't be able to count all the people in your great big family either! Your brand-new name will be Abraham, which means *the father of many*. Your wife's new name will be Sarah. And I won't just give you and Sarah a son. I will give you grandsons and granddaughters, great-grandchildren and great-great-grandchildren. One day, *your* family will be the biggest, the most wonderful family in the whole world!" Abraham clapped his hands in delight. And even though he and his wife were almost a hundred years old, if God had promised that they would have a son, Abraham believed it.

Now, what do you think happened? One day, Sarah and Abraham did have a baby boy! They called him Isaac, whose name means *laughter*. That baby boy would grow up to have two sons of his own and twelve grandsons! Abraham's family kept growing and growing, until one day, the most famous son the world has ever known was born into Abraham's family. That son was Jesus. God had taken Abraham's small-sized dream and made it into a God-sized dream. And God-sized dreams are always the very best ones to have.

God-sized Dreams Are Best!

Do you have dreams for your life? When you close your eyes, what do you hope for the future? Whatever it is, God has a bigger, better, and far more wonderful dream for you! As you pray to God, ask him to show you what his dream for you might be. Ask him to help you discover all the wonderful dreams and plans he has for you—because God's big dreams for you are amazing!

Dear God,
Thank you for the wonderful
dreams and plans you have for me.
Help me to find out what they are.
Amen.

I know the plans I have for you.

JEREMIAH 29:11

In the Desert

GENESIS 28:10–22

It was night. The huge orange sun sank low behind the mountains, leaving a hot, fiery glow on the desert floor. Abraham's grandson was glad. Perhaps now he could rest. Jacob had been running all day, trying to escape from the brother he had cheated. He might never be able to go home now.

Darkness fell as Jacob tried to sleep. What a horrible place this was! The dry desert wind whipped around him as he laid his head on the hard stone. It was the only thing he could find for a pillow.

As he closed his eyes, he saw something he couldn't believe. The clouds above his head opened, and a huge golden staircase came down from heaven and touched the floor. Angels floated up and down the stairs, and at the very top of the golden staircase stood God himself. And then, as if that wasn't amazing enough, God spoke.

"Jacob, I am the God of your grandfather, Abraham; the God of your father, Isaac. One day, you will come back to your home. I will give to you all the land on which you are lying. Your family will be the biggest, the best, and the most wonderful family in the whole world. Trust me. I will keep my promises."

Jacob jumped for joy. He recognized that promise! That was
the very same promise God had given to his grandpa Abraham all
those years ago! God was right here, in the desert, after all. Jacob
threw off his cloak, sprang up, took the stone that had been his
pillow, and made it into a memorial. He poured oil over the stone,
then he knelt on the sand and prayed. "Awesome God, I know
you are in this place. Thank you for being with me on this journey
and watching over me. You are my God. Thank you that you are a
promise maker and a promise keeper. Amen."

Many years later, Jacob would come home and make things right
with his brother. Jacob's family grew and became great, just like
God said it would. God had kept his wonderful promise. Because he
always does.

God Is *Your* Promise Maker and *Your* Promise Keeper

One of the most wonderful things about God is that he is *everywhere*. Just like God was in the desert with Jacob, God is with *you*. Wherever you go, whatever you experience, God is watching over your life, just waiting to keep his promises to you. God is *your* promise maker and *your* promise keeper. And that means that you can make Jacob's prayer *your* prayer too.

Awesome God,
I know you are in this place.
Thank you for being with me on this journey
and watching over me. You are my God.
Thank you that you are a promise maker
and a promise keeper.
Amen.

---

*I will not leave you until I have done
what I have promised you.*

GENESIS 28:15

Around the Fire

EXODUS 4, 3:1–12

It was quiet on the mountainside. The only noise was the sound of the wind as it whispered through the trees and rustled the leaves. Moses leaned on his shepherd's staff and watched the sheep as they nibbled the grass. Out of the corner of his eye, Moses caught sight of something orange and red dancing in the distance. A bush was on fire! Moses quickly walked toward the bush. It was covered in flames, but the leaves were still green! And suddenly, from out of the burning bush, came a voice.

"Moses! Moses! Take off your shoes. You are standing on holy ground. I am the God of your father, the God of Abraham, the God of Isaac and the God of Jacob." Moses could hardly believe it—God was talking to *him*, in the middle of the desert, through a burning bush! Moses quickly bent down, took off his sandals, and covered his eyes. What could God want with him?

"I have a special job for you, Moses," said God. "I'm sending you to Egypt, where the Israelites are kept as slaves. Go to Pharaoh, the king, and tell him to let my people go. I have chosen *you* to bring them out of Egypt."

Moses nearly fainted with fear. How could he do what God was asking? Pharaoh was strong, powerful, and cruel, with a heart as hard as stone. Moses was a quiet, humble shepherd.

How could he hope to change Pharaoh's heart? Moses asked question after question. What if the Israelites didn't believe that God had sent him? Suppose he got his words all mixed up? What if everything went wrong? Finally, Moses simply said, "I can't do it."

But did you know that when we say *I can't*, God says *I can*?

"Moses," said God quietly. "*I* will be with you. *I* will give you the words to say. *I* will teach you what to do."

Moses stopped talking, and started trusting. He stopped pouting, and started praying. As those orange flames flickered and danced around the bush, Moses knew that what he *couldn't* do, God *could*.

Moses picked up his sandals, put them on his feet, and set off toward Egypt. He did not walk alone. God, the one who could do *all* things, was walking beside him.

What We Can't Do, God Can

What would you say if God asked you to do something you thought you couldn't do? Would you have questions for God like Moses did? Of course you would. But if God asks us to do something, no matter how hard it might be, we need to trust. We need to pray. And when we trust and pray, an amazing thing happens. We come to understand that what *we* can't do, *God* can.

Dear God,
Thank you for showing me there is *nothing* you can't do.
Help me to trust you, to pray hard, and work hard,
so that I'll be able to do everything you ask.
Amen.

With God, all things are possible.

MATTHEW 19:26

By the Sea

Moses closed his eyes and tried not to panic. It was less than a year since he stood in front of the burning bush, trembling and terrified. But the fear he had felt that day was nothing compared to this. How was God going to save him and the Israelites now? They were trapped! Behind them stood Pharaoh's huge army—over six hundred chariots and thousands of soldiers. In front of them lay the deep, mighty waters of the Red Sea. There was no escape.

"Save us, Moses!" the people cried. "Have you brought us out of Egypt to drown in the sea?"

Moses knew this was his biggest test yet. He could panic, or he could pray. He could tremble, or he could trust. Moses chose to trust. He knew without a doubt that God was awesome and mighty. He had been filled with awe and wonder as he watched what happened when Pharaoh refused to let the Israelites go. Moses would never forget how God brought those ten terrible plagues upon Egypt—the nasty flies that covered the land, the frogs that hopped everywhere, and the mighty hailstorm. He remembered how God protected the Israelites as they fled from Egypt, covering them with a pillar of cloud by day and a pillar of fire by night. God would not leave them now. Moses was sure of it. Standing on the bank of the Red Sea, Moses had nowhere to turn. So Moses turned to God.

"We're not going to be afraid!" Moses shouted to the people. "We're going to stand still and see what the Lord will do!"

The trouble was, Moses didn't know what God was going to do. And neither did anyone else. But God loves to surprise us in unexpected ways.

"Moses, hold out your staff over the sea," God commanded. No sooner had Moses stretched out his hand than a strong east wind began to blow on the waters. As Moses watched in amazement, a path opened up right in the middle of the sea and the Israelites charged forward to escape from Pharaoh and his mighty army. As soon as God's people all safely crossed to the other side, the water came rushing back, and the chariots disappeared under the waves.

The Israelites were safe. Moses had trusted in God, and God had stepped in at just the right time. That night, the Israelites sang and feasted and danced for joy. And early in the morning, they set out on their journey toward the promised land. God was on their side, and nothing could stop them.

Stand Still

Can you imagine how scary it was for Moses to stand on the banks of the Red Sea when it looked like there was no escape? But Moses knew that he had done everything he could—the rest was up to God. Sometimes, after we've prayed about a situation and done everything we can, we just need to be still and see what God will do. Our great God, who can make a path through the sea, loves to do things we never expect. So when you have nowhere to turn, turn to God. Stand still. Don't panic—just pray; don't tremble—just trust. And get ready to be surprised.

Dear God,
Help me to remember that I can turn to you
and trust you in every situation. Help me to be still,
and watch for the surprising things you will do.
Amen.

*So stand still. Watch the great thing
the Lord is about to do right here in front of you!*

1 SAMUEL 12:16

Around the City

The closer the Israelites got to Jericho, the smaller they felt. There was no way they could get inside that city. The walls were huge! The big, solid gates were locked tight—no one was going in, and no one was coming out. But their leader, Joshua, refused to be afraid. As he stood looking up at the massive walls, Joshua thought about all the wonderful words God had whispered to him.

I'll never leave you, Joshua. Be strong and brave. I'm going with you into this new place, and everywhere you place your foot, the land will be yours. I've given this city to you already.

How amazing! Joshua could be confident that Jericho would belong to the Israelites—because God had already given it to them. He just had to convince the people of that.

"How are we going to get in there, Joshua?" the Israelites cried. "We need a battering ram!" But Joshua smiled. They didn't need a battering ram. They just needed prayer.

"We're going to march around the city and blow trumpets," said Joshua, as the Israelites stared at him in amazement. "And no talking."

Joshua took the first step and everyone else followed. Round the wall the Israelites marched. And every day for six days, they circled the city once, never making even the smallest peep. But the trumpets kept blowing and Joshua kept going. He knew that with every step he took, and with every circle he completed, he was stepping toward God's promise.

On the seventh day, the Israelites circled the city six times as the priests blew their trumpets. On the seventh time around the walls, with a loud trumpet blast, all the Israelites gave a huge cry, and guess what happened? The walls of Jericho came tumbling down! With a shriek and a shout, the Israelites poured into the city, leaping and laughing and cheering for God. Joshua shook his head in amazement as he looked at the once-mighty stones that lay at his feet. It was a miracle. Jericho belonged to the Israelites. But all the glory belonged to God.

Circle Your Prayer

Don't you wish you could have been there the day the walls of Jericho came tumbling down? It must have been an amazing sight to see! Who would have thought those walls would come crashing down just because the Israelites kept circling the city? But Joshua knew that prayer is stronger than any battering ram. When we pray continually and confidently—over and over about something—that's just like drawing a big circle around our prayer. And as we keep praying every day, it's like saying, *I know you can do this, God. I believe in the power of prayer.* And you can be confident, like Joshua was, that God will give you an answer.

Dear God,
Thank you that I can be confident when I pray to you,
just like Joshua was. Help me to be a circle maker—
to keep praying and circling your promises to me,
like those Israelites did all those years ago.
Amen.

Here is what we can be sure of when we come to God in prayer.
If we ask anything in keeping with what he wants, he hears us.
If we know that God hears what we ask for, we know that we have it.

1 JOHN 5:14–15

In the Temple

1 SAMUEL 1—2:11

Hannah's knees were sore and her heart was heavy. But she would not give up. She would keep kneeling on the floor until she was sure that God heard her prayer.

For years and years, Hannah had prayed for a son, but she still wasn't a mother. A baby boy was the one thing she wanted more than anything else in the world. Hannah bowed her head as her tears fell quietly to the floor.

"Please, God, please," Hannah whispered. "Don't forget about me. If you will give me a son, I promise to bring him back here, to your temple, where he can work for you."

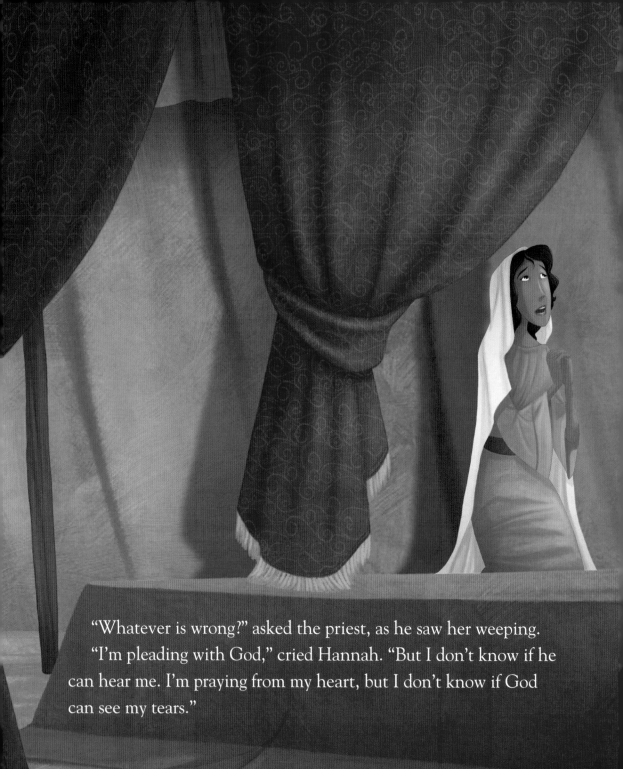

"Whatever is wrong?" asked the priest, as he saw her weeping.

"I'm pleading with God," cried Hannah. "But I don't know if he can hear me. I'm praying from my heart, but I don't know if God can see my tears."

But God *could* hear Hannah's prayer. And not only could he see her tears, he was catching them as they fell. Hannah's tears did not fall to the floor. They fell into God's hand.

"Go in peace," said the priest, "and may God grant what you asked."

One year later, Hannah's heart burst with joy as she held her baby son. She called him Samuel, which means *I asked the Lord for him*.

And when Samuel was three years old, Hannah took him back to the temple to live with the priest and work for God, just as she had promised.

This time, Hannah's tears were tears of joy. "I'm the woman who was crying here all those years ago," she said to the priest. "God did not forget me. God heard my prayer. Here is the son God gave me. Help him to serve the Lord."

When Hannah got home, she knelt in prayer. But this time it was a prayer of praise, to the One who heard her cries and caught her tears in his hand.

God Listens to Your Heart

God is always with us. He feels our joy and our pain. When you are hurting, try to remember that God sees your tears and catches them as they fall. God cares about you so much that when you cry, he cries too. God listens to every cry of your heart. He never forgets about you. And he has promised that one day, he will wipe away every tear from our eyes. What a wonderful day that will be!

Dear God,
Thank you that you never forget about me,
even when I feel alone. Help me to remember
that you listen to the cries of my heart.
Amen.

List my tears in your book.
Aren't you making a record of them?

PSALM 56:8

In the Fields

PSALM 23

It was dark. All David's little lambs were curled up, fast asleep. The shepherd boy lay on his back in the field and gazed at the stars as they twinkled overhead. David knew that just like he watched over his sheep, God was watching over him. And in the darkness, David sang his prayer to God:

God, you are my shepherd and I'm your precious sheep.

You give me everything I need—water, food, and sleep.

You lead me on the safest paths, you'll always be guide.

And even when the valley's dark, I know you're by my side.

You spread a feast in front of me, my cup will overflow.

And your great love and goodness will follow where I go.

David fell asleep under the stars. He didn't need a blanket.
He was covered in God's blessings. They were enough.

God's Blessings Follow Us

Has someone ever filled your cup so much that it overflowed? That's what God does with his blessings. God just loves to pour good things into your life, and his blessings never run out. That's what David discovered when he wrote his song of praise, and that's what you will discover when you spend time in prayer. You can never hide from God's love and goodness—they will follow you wherever you go.

Dear God,
Thank you that your love and goodness
cover me like a warm blanket and follow me wherever I go.
Thank you that your blessings never run out.
Amen.

---

*I am sure that your goodness and love
will follow me all the days of my life.*

PSALM 23:6

In the Valley

1 SAMUEL 17

David stood in the tent and peeked out at King Saul from under a huge helmet. It was too big for David's head and drooped over his eyes. The coat of armor King Saul gave him didn't fit either. The sword was much too heavy for the little shepherd boy to carry. "I'm sorry, King Saul," said David. "But I can't wear this armor of yours. It's too big. And besides, I don't need it."

"What do you mean?" spluttered King Saul, as David laid his armor on the ground. "That giant out there is over nine feet tall. He's bigger than any man I've ever seen. He's the most powerful warrior in the whole Philistine army. He could stand on you and squash you flat. You need protection."

"King Saul," the little shepherd boy replied. "Don't you know that God is bigger and stronger than any giant? God has helped me fight off a lion and a bear. He'll help me fight Goliath." And with that, David picked up his shepherd's sling, found five smooth stones, and marched out onto the battlefield to face Goliath.

The giant *was* huge. The monster of a man stood in the valley, blocking out the sun and roaring at the top of his voice. "They sent a *boy* to fight me?" he bellowed. "A *boy*! Come over here and I'll feed you to the birds!"

David was not afraid. "You might have your sword, Goliath," he shouted back. "But I have my God, who is bigger and stronger and greater than any giant!" As Goliath moved closer and opened his huge mouth to laugh, David quickly loaded his slingshot and fired just one smooth stone toward the giant. It hit Goliath straight between the eyes, and immediately the giant fell to the ground, dead.

Everyone watching was shocked. The Philistine army turned around and ran away, and King Saul shook his head in amazement. David was the only one who wasn't surprised at what happened that day. The little shepherd boy had known all along that God was bigger than any giant. David put his slingshot back in his pocket, picked up his shepherd's staff, and set off back to the fields where his sheep were waiting.

God Is Bigger than Your Biggest Problem

Do you believe that God is bigger than your biggest problem? He is! Think about David, that little shepherd boy, looking after his sheep in the fields at night. Lions and bears would have been a big problem. Imagine them creeping up in the dark to steal David's lambs. But David knew that God is bigger than any bear. David knew that God is larger than any lion. And when David marched out to face Goliath, he knew that God is greater than any giant. Do you believe that too? When you have a problem, ask God to help you with it. Trust him. He can handle anything.

Dear God,
When I'm facing a problem,
help me to remember that you are bigger
and stronger than anything I'm afraid of.
Help me to trust you.
Amen.

Great is our Lord. His power is mighty.

PSALM 147:5

On the Mountain

1 KINGS 18:1, 41–45

It had not rained in Israel for three long years. Every blade of grass was gone, every tree was withered, every animal was thin, and every person was thirsty. Israel was a desert. The springs were dry, the valleys were dry, the fields were dry, and the earth was dry. Cracks opened up and slithered like snakes across the dusty ground. Nothing could grow and nothing could flourish.

But Elijah knew that rain was coming. He knew it because God had told him so. After all those years of listening to God and bringing God's message to the people, Elijah knew without a doubt that when God made a promise, it would be kept.

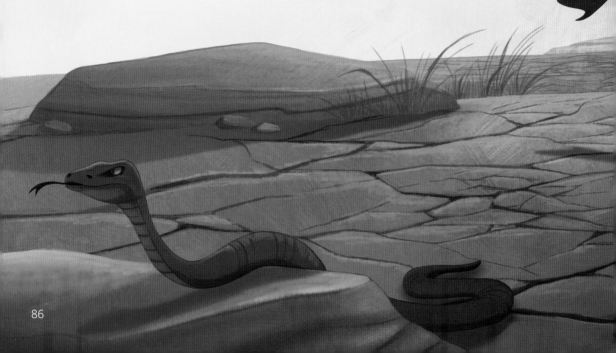

Elijah and his servant climbed wearily up the slopes of Mount Carmel, where Elijah sank to his knees in the dust. Elijah put his head down to the ground and prayed for the promise he knew would be kept. "Go and look toward the sea," he told his servant. "For I can hear the rain."

But even though the servant scanned the horizon, he could see no rain. Even though he turned his ear toward the sea, he could hear no rain.

"There's nothing there, Elijah," the servant reported.

"Then go back," said Elijah, still on his knees, praying.

The servant looked again, but could see nothing different—only the same, hot, relentless sun beating down on Israel's dry and dusty land.

"You're wrong, Elijah," the servant said. "There is no rain."

"But there *will* be rain!" Elijah cried. "Just keep looking. Just keep listening."

Seven times, Elijah prayed. Seven times, he sent his servant to look out over the sea. And after the seventh time, the servant came back and said, "Elijah, I see the smallest cloud in the sky. It's only the size of a man's hand. Could that be rain? I hear the faintest whisper in the air. Could that be rain?"

Elijah jumped up. And there, sure enough, was a tiny rain cloud, being carried toward them on the wind. And as they listened closely, Elijah and his servant could hear the sweet and certain sound of raindrops as they danced on the ocean. "That's it!" cried Elijah. "Tell the king to take his chariot and his horse and flee before the rain comes."

And when the rain came, it was not just a drizzle. Huge, dark clouds filled the sky as torrents of rain poured from heaven over the land. It filled every valley and every spring and every crack in the dry ground, until the grass turned green and the flowers popped out their heads to drink.

Elijah tucked his cloak into his belt and set off down the mountain, running in the rain, and giving thanks to the one who had kept his promise.

Keep Looking, Keep Listening

I wonder if Elijah's servant really believed the rain would come that day. Seven times, he had to go back; seven times, he kept looking and listening for that rain. And when he saw the cloud, it was so small! When you pray to God, watch out for the small things he might be doing—because sometimes they are easy to miss. Keep listening for his quiet voice—because sometimes it might be hard to hear. Keep praying—because the more you pray, the more you'll notice. Keep looking for what God is doing, and keep listening for his whisper. You'll see it. You'll hear it.

Help me, God,
to have faith in your promises; to keep praying,
to keep looking for what you will do in my life,
and to keep listening for your whispers to me.
Amen.

Be still, and know that I am God.

PSALM 46:10

Before the Battle

2 CHRONICLES 20:1–29

King Jehoshaphat had a problem. His people had a problem. They knelt on the floor in front of him and wailed, "Oh, King! Did you hear the terrible news? There's a massive army marching toward us and we don't stand a chance. What shall we do?"

King Jehoshaphat didn't know what to do. The army descending on them was much bigger than his own. His best battle plan could not save them. But God could—King Jehoshaphat was sure of it. He didn't know *how* God would help them win, but he would praise him for it anyway—before the battle had even been fought.

King Jehoshaphat stood up. "People of Judah," he said loudly. "We're not going to be defeated. We serve a great and mighty God. Let's praise him for what he will do. Bow your heads with me and pray."

A hush fell on the temple as all the people bowed their heads to listen to their king. And King Jehoshaphat prayed the most powerful prayer of his life.

Lord, you are the God of our people. You are God of heaven and earth. You alone are strong, and powerful, and mighty. No one can fight against you and win. You have saved our people before, and you will save us now. We don't know how, but we know without doubt you'll do it. Amen.

As soon as King Jehoshaphat finished praying, the prophet Jahaziel jumped up. "Don't be afraid!" he cried. "Don't lose hope! Go out and face this army tomorrow. The battle is not yours—it's God's!"

Early the next morning, King Jehoshaphat assembled his army. But before they set off, he marched to the front of the line with his very best singers. "Sing to the Lord as we march," said the king, "Sing as loud as you can. Let's praise God for what he will do today!" So King Jehoshaphat's army set off, with his little singing band in the lead.

When they reached the battlefield, to everyone's amazement, everything was quiet. There were no men banging their swords against shields. There were no soldiers waiting to jump out at them. "Where are our enemies?" asked Jehoshaphat as he looked around. But they were gone. God had caused those armies to battle against each other, and there was no one left for King Jehoshaphat to fight.

"Bring out the harps!" cried King Jehoshaphat, as he clapped his hands in delight. "Bring out the trumpets! Let's celebrate our awesome God who won this battle for us!"

And that is just what they did. King Jehoshaphat and his people danced until the stars came out. His little singing band sang so loudly that in the morning, their throats were sore. But it was worth it.

Don't Just Pray Through— Praise Through

Don't we have an awesome God? God loves it when we are confident that he's on our side, like King Jehoshaphat was. And here's a little secret: when you're facing something hard, like a battle or a problem you think is impossible to get through, don't just pray through it—*praise* through it. Pray like King Jehoshaphat did. Say: *God, this battle belongs to you. I don't know how you're going to help me through this situation, but I know you will, and I'm going to praise you anyway.* God loves it when we pray like that, and it will make *you* feel better too. You can put that problem right into God's hands—there's no better place for it.

Dear God,
When I'm facing a tough situation,
help me to praise you as I pray.
Amen.

Put your hope in God. Once again I will have reason to praise him. He is my Savior and my God.

PSALM 42:5

In the Pit

DANIEL 6

Daniel knew he was being watched as he knelt by his open window to pray. He could see the sunlight glinting off two bald heads belonging to the advisors of King Darius as they spied on him. But it didn't matter to Daniel. He'd been dropping to his knees and praying to God three times a day ever since he could remember. He wasn't going to stop now. Even when he saw the advisors scurrying off to the palace to report him to the Persian king, Daniel still kept praying.

"King Darius!" the bald-headed advisors gasped as they ran into the throne room. "You'll never guess what just happened. The man you wanted to put in charge of the whole kingdom has broken the law that you yourself signed. No one is supposed to pray to *anyone* except you for thirty days. But we just saw Daniel, on his knees, at his open window, praying to his God! That can only mean one thing, Your Majesty—Daniel must be thrown to the lions."

King Darius had signed that law only a few days before. It seemed like a good idea at the time, but now the king realized he had been tricked by the two men who stood before him. They had wanted to get rid of Daniel all along. "Are you sure you're not mistaken?" asked King Darius. "There's no mistake about it, Your Majesty," the scheming advisors replied. "The law cannot be changed. You must stick to your word."

May your God save you, Daniel," the king cried. Then Daniel was thrown into the pit where several hungry lions were lying in wait for their supper.

That night, the king could hardly sleep. He tossed and turned in bed, hoping that Daniel's God would save him. At the first sign of sunrise, he rushed out of the palace and ran to the edge of the pit to see if Daniel was still alive. "Daniel!" the king shouted into the large space below. "Daniel, are you there? Did your God save you?" And amazingly, Daniel's voice called out, "Yes, Your Majesty. He did! My God sent his angel to save me. He shut the mouths of the lions and I don't have a scratch on me."

King Darius jumped for joy. He ordered
Daniel to be lifted from the pit and wrote a
decree to all the nations that said:

You must praise the living God
Who rules both day and night.
He is the one who frees and saves
With glory, power, and might.

And Daniel went home, climbed the
stairs to his room, opened his window, and
knelt down to pray.

Stop, Drop, and Pray

What do you suppose Daniel did when he was thrown into that pit? Don't you think he must have prayed right away? He must have dropped straight to his knees and pleaded with God to save him. But Daniel didn't just pray when he had a bad day; he prayed every day—three times a day. Whatever he was doing, whatever kind of day he was having, Daniel stopped, dropped to his knees, and prayed. Is prayer a habit in your life? If not, try to make it one. Stop, drop, and pray!

Dear God,
Help me to develop a habit
of praying to you every day.
Amen.

At all times, pray by the power of the Spirit.
Pray all kinds of prayers. Be watchful,
so that you can pray. Always keep on praying.

EPHESIANS 6:18

In the Fish

In his bunk below deck, Jonah put his head in his hands. This was not a good situation. The boat heaved up and down as the mighty waves tossed it around in the ocean. What a terrible idea of his to try to run away from God. What an even worse idea to get on board this ship! He should have done what God wanted him to. He should have gone to Nineveh, that wicked town, and given God's message to the people there. But it was too late now.

"Jonah!" the sailors yelled. "Is this storm your fault? Where are you from? What's happening?" Jonah knew there was only one thing to do. "It *is* my fault!" he shouted. "I'm trying to run away from God, and I know I shouldn't be here. Throw me overboard!"

The sailors were terrified! They tried hard to row back to shore, but it was no use. The storm was too strong. Eventually, they picked Jonah up and threw him overboard. Jonah sank— down, down, down, into the deep waters until suddenly, he felt as if he was being pulled by a very strong current. What was happening?

To Jonah's horror, he realized he was inside a huge fish, as seaweed, dead fish, and an octopus floated by his head. Oh no! If he thought Nineveh was a bad place, then this was ten times worse. Jonah did the only thing he could do. He prayed.

Dear God, here I am in the depths of the ocean. I have sunk lower than I ever thought possible. But even so, I know you are listening. I know I'm never too far away for you to hear my prayer. I know you will save me. And when you do, I will go to Nineveh. Amen.

As soon as Jonah finished praying, he felt himself being carried up, and up, and up, until suddenly, the fish gave a giant hiccup and spat him out onto the beach. Jonah lay on the sand in shock. And when he had recovered, he set off for Nineveh.

▼

God Hears *Every* Prayer and Answers *Every* Cry

Can you imagine how awful it must have been for Jonah to be inside that fish? Sitting there in the darkness, trapped inside a huge belly, thousands of feet beneath the waves; he must have felt so far away from God. He must have wondered if God *really* could hear his prayer. But God did. No matter how far we travel, no matter how dark it seems, no matter what is going on around us—God hears *every* prayer, and answers *every* cry.

Dear God,
How wonderful to know that no matter where I am,
or what is going on in my life, you *always* hear my prayer,
and answer every cry. Help me to remember that truth.
Amen.

I call out to God ... and he hears my voice.

PSALM 55:16–17

New Testament

With the Angel

LUKE 1:26–56, LUKE 2:20

It was just another ordinary day for Mary—until the angel came. She had cleaned the house and made supper, swept the floor and baked bread. Then all at once, out of nowhere, an angel stepped into Mary's ordinary day, and announced something extraordinary.

"You are blessed, Mary," the angel whispered. "You're going to have a baby."

"How can that possibly be?" Mary stuttered, as her mind flooded with questions. She was just a young girl. She wasn't even married to Joseph yet. What would he say? What would her parents say? How could this happen? But the angel just kept smiling. "Your baby will be God's own son, and one day he'll be a king. You must name him *Jesus*, because he will save everyone from their sins. Don't be afraid. Just believe that nothing is impossible with God."

Mary kneeled and looked at
the angel standing in front of her.
"I'm God's servant," she whispered
quietly. "I trust him." And with
that, Mary knelt down, bowed her
head, and softly said a prayer.

Who am I, to be so blessed,

To hear you call my name?

To stand where angels visit me,

And never be the same?

Who am I, to be so blessed—

The momma of God's son?

May it be just as you said,

And let the promise come.

Nine months later, in a little starlit stable in Bethlehem, Mary looked down at the tiny treasure she rocked in her arms, this perfect promise from God—Jesus. As Mary gazed at her sleeping son, she thought about all that had happened since the angel's visit, and the wonderful words he had said. How amazing that one day, this little baby would become a king. How awesome that Jesus had come into the world to save everyone from their sins. Mary didn't know how Jesus would do that, but in the stillness of that Bethlehem night, she wasn't looking for answers. Mary was looking for God. And wasn't God everywhere to be found? In the face of her baby, in the star shining through the window, in the eyes of the smiling shepherds, in the quiet voice of Joseph—God was there. And God could always be trusted.

As Mary placed her little one in the manger, she knew that from this moment on, she would never have an ordinary day again.

Don't Look for Answers; Look for God

Did you know that Mary was only a young teenager when the angel came? That must have been frightening. But did you see what Mary did? All along, Mary trusted God. When she found herself wondering about the future, she decided not to look for the answers herself, but to look for God instead. And she found him. God was all around her, and God is all around *you* too. So if you have questions, pray about it; don't look for the answers—look for God.

Dear God,
When I have questions, or I wonder about
what might happen in the future, help me to look for you.
Thank you that through it all, I can trust you.
Amen.

We don't know what to do.
But we're looking to you to help us.

2 CHRONICLES 20:12

In the River

LUKE 3:2–22

John the Baptist dipped the last of the locusts into his honey, quickly finished his lunch, and set off running through the desert. He had heard a voice. And it was no ordinary voice. It was God's voice. And John knew exactly what he was supposed to do.

It didn't take him long to reach the Jordan River. In John jumped, up to his waist, as the people around him stared. "Are you ready?" cried John. "Are you ready to listen to God? Are you ready to change your ways, to share your food and your clothes? Are you

ready to help others? If you are, now is your chance to show it. Jump into the river with me. Be baptized!" And they did. All the people who were ready for a new start jumped into the cold water. When they emerged, they asked John, "Are you the Messiah? Are you the one who God sent, the one who will save us all?"

"No," said John. "I'm just the messenger. My job is to help you get ready for him. I baptize you with water, but that can only make you clean on the outside. When the Messiah comes, he'll help you be clean on the inside too. You will feel like you have brand-new hearts."

And then, one quiet morning when the time was right, Jesus came right up to John as he was standing in the Jordan River. "I'm ready to be baptized," Jesus said. Even though John felt he wasn't good enough to do it, he obeyed, and plunged Jesus down under the cold water.

When Jesus came up out of the river, he prayed, and something amazing happened. The doors of heaven burst open and a beautiful white dove flew gently down and landed on Jesus' head. God's Holy Spirit was hovering right there, above the Son of God as he stood in the river. God himself smiled down and said, "This is my Son. I am pleased with him."

That was just the beginning. God's Son stepped out from the river and into the world—he was ready to help people have brand-new hearts.

Prayer Opens Heaven

Did you notice what happened when Jesus prayed? Find Luke 3:21 in your Bible and read it. It says that when Jesus prayed, heaven was opened. Wow—what a beautiful image! Perhaps if heaven has gates, those gates swing open when we pray. If heaven has doors, perhaps the doors open wide when we pray. And if heaven lies beyond the clouds, maybe the clouds move aside when we pray. Can you see those pictures in your mind? Think about that the next time you talk with God— you're knocking on heaven's doors, and when you pray, your prayers open heaven!

Dear God,
Thank you for the beautiful picture I have in my mind—
that when I pray to you, heaven is opened.
Help me to remember that every time I talk to you.
Amen.

Knock, and the door will be opened to you.

MATTHEW 7:7

On the Hillside

MATTHEW 6:5–15; LUKE 11:1

"Master," the disciples said to Jesus, "teach us to pray."

Sheep grazed quietly on the hillside above the Sea of Galilee. The green grass felt like a thick, comfy cushion. The disciples leaned back, ready to listen to Jesus. They knew he prayed all the time. Often, when the mornings were still dark and the disciples still sleepy, Jesus was wide awake and had climbed the hillside to pray. "This is how you should pray," Jesus said. And he looked up to the sky and began …

Our Father, who lives in heaven,
Holy is your name.
May what **you** want always be done …
On earth, in heaven—the same.
Give us the food we need each day.
Forgive us each mistake,
And help us be forgivers too
At every turn we make.
Lead us down a path that's right,
That helps us find our way,
And save us, God, from doing wrong,
Each and every day. Amen.

The words of Jesus' prayer hung in the stillness. It was the simplest, most powerful prayer the disciples had ever heard. It was a prayer that would reach far beyond their lifetimes, and travel into every corner of the world.

Pray the Prayer of Jesus

Did you know that the little prayer Jesus taught his disciples is still being said by millions and millions of people all around the world? Did you know that the words of that prayer have been translated into hundreds of languages? Every Sunday, when Christians gather to worship, the Lord's Prayer is read, or sung, or whispered, from the north to the south, from the east to the west. What a wonderful prayer Jesus taught us! Let's pray ...

Our Father in heaven,
may your name be honored.
May your kingdom come.
May what you want to happen be done
on earth as it is done in heaven.
Give us today our daily bread.
And forgive us our sins,
just as we also have forgiven those who sin against us.
Keep us from sinning when we are tempted.
Save us from the evil one.
Amen.

MATTHEW 6:9–13

In the Crowd

JOHN 6:1–13

It was an impossible situation. Philip knew it. Andrew knew it. All the disciples knew it. What was Jesus thinking? Gathered in front of them on the hillside was a huge crowd of people. There had to be over five thousand! And here was Jesus, asking the disciples to find dinner for them all. How ridiculous!

Philip felt helpless. "Jesus!" he exclaimed. "If I worked for eight months, I still wouldn't have enough money to buy bread for all these people!"

Andrew felt embarrassed. It was kind of a little boy to offer to share his lunch, but what would Jesus think when he looked in the basket? This was a big problem. Five small loaves and two tiny fish was only enough for one boy, not over five thousand people!

But Jesus felt wonderful. "Have the people sit down," he said quietly. A hush fell on the hillside as more than five thousand hungry people fixed their eyes on Jesus and waited. Jesus took the boy's basket and lifted it to the heavens. His prayer was only two tiny words. "Thank you."

And then came the miracle. Philip, Andrew, and the little boy watched in amazement as that tiny lunch fed every single person on the hillside. The five loaves and two little fish became enough for more than five thousand people. And soon, every single person was full. There was plenty for seconds, thirds, fourths—and more besides!

As evening came and Andrew and Philip made their way down the hillside, they shook their heads in wonder. They still had so much to learn! Jesus had taken five little loaves and two tiny fish and multiplied them to feed *five thousand* people. Jesus had taken an impossible situation and turned it around with one tiny prayer. He had looked in the basket, and instead of seeing a problem, Jesus saw possibility. And if Jesus could take one little lunch and turn it into a fantastic feast, surely there was *nothing* he could not do.

God Loves to Multiply

How many people can eat five loaves of bread and two tiny fish? One person, maybe two. But when God is hosting the party, it's enough for five thousand people! You see, God loves to multiply. God can take the little bit that you give and multiply it so that it becomes something much, much greater! So whatever small thing you are ready to share with others—whether it's your time, or your prayers, or your money—get ready to pray, just like Jesus did. Say, *Thank you, God.* Then watch for the amazing things he will do!

Dear God,
Thank you that you can take whatever
I have to give, and do amazing things with it.
Amen.

*God is able to do far more
than we could ever ask for or imagine.*

EPHESIANS 3:20

On the Road

MATTHEW 8:5–13

The Roman commander strode quickly and purposefully through the streets of Capernaum, his cloak blowing behind him. He had to see Jesus. This would not wait. He knew without doubt that Jesus could heal his servant. All he had to do was ask.

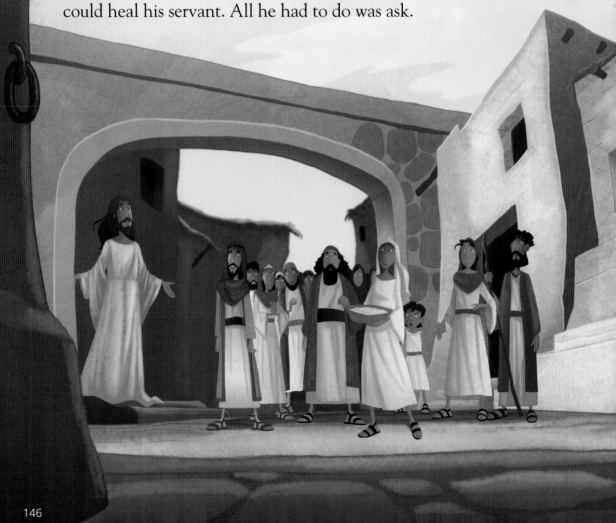

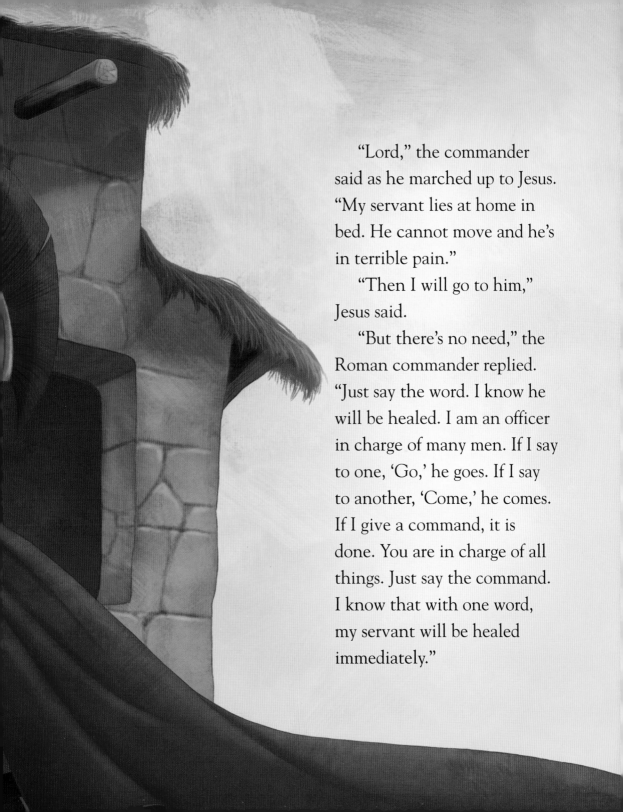

"Lord," the commander said as he marched up to Jesus. "My servant lies at home in bed. He cannot move and he's in terrible pain."

"Then I will go to him," Jesus said.

"But there's no need," the Roman commander replied. "Just say the word. I know he will be healed. I am an officer in charge of many men. If I say to one, 'Go,' he goes. If I say to another, 'Come,' he comes. If I give a command, it is done. You are in charge of all things. Just say the command. I know that with one word, my servant will be healed immediately."

Jesus was completely and utterly amazed. Never had he heard such a bold request. He turned to his disciples and all the crowd behind him and said, "Do you see this man? He has the greatest faith I have ever seen in the whole of Israel!" And turning back to the Roman commander, Jesus smiled and said, "Go. It will be done just as you believed it would be. Your servant will be healed." And he was.

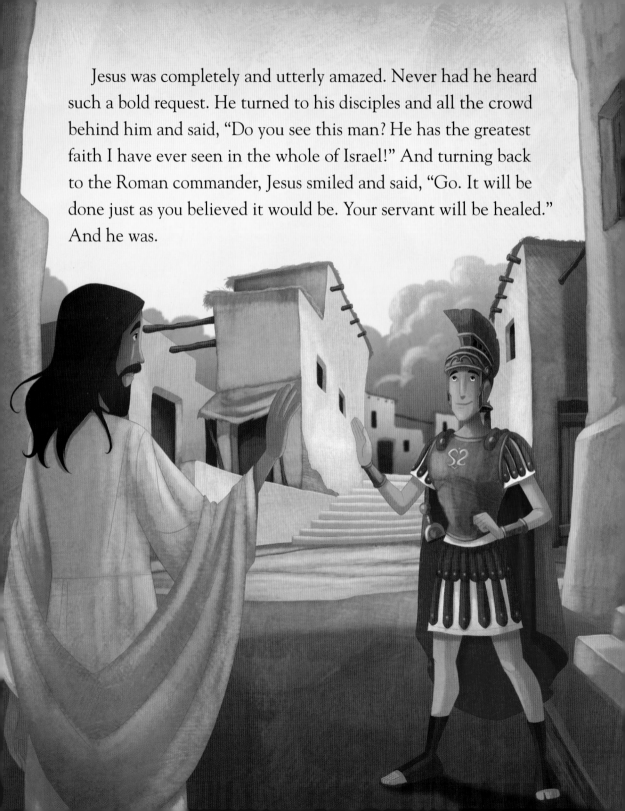

God Loves Bold Prayers

There's a beautiful picture in the Bible of God sitting on a throne. He's waiting there to hear your prayers; he's watching to see who has faith in him. And the bigger and bolder your prayers, the more God loves to hear them. So just like that commander marched up to Jesus, you can march up to God with confidence; you can kneel before his throne and pray the biggest, boldest prayer ever. God, who is in charge of all things, is not afraid of big, bold prayers. In fact, God loves them, because it shows that you have faith in what our big God can do!

Dear God,
Thank you that I can come to you
with confidence when I pray.
Help me to remember that no prayer
is too big, or too bold, for you to answer.
Amen.

So let us boldly approach God's throne of grace.

HEBREWS 4:16

In the Dark

MARK 10:46–52

Bartimaeus sat by the side of the road. A big yellow sun rose high over the streets of Jericho, round and bright and warm. Birds twittered and flew in the blue sky above and landed on the branches of the trees as they nodded in the wind. But Bartimaeus could not see the sun, or the trees, or the birds that perched on their branches. He was blind. Every day was dark for Bartimaeus. Until the day Jesus came to town.

"Jesus! Jesus! Have mercy on me!" he cried as he heard Jesus coming down the road with his disciples. "Be quiet!" the people said. But Bartimaeus knew about Jesus. If anyone could answer his prayer, it was this man. So he cried out again, even louder this time. "Jesus! Jesus! Help me!"

Jesus stopped. "Tell him to come to me," he said.

"Cheer up, Bartimaeus," the people said. "He's calling for you."
Bartimaeus threw off his coat, jumped up, and came to Jesus. "What
do you want me to do for you?" Jesus asked.

"Lord," Bartimaeus said quietly. "I want to see."

All the people standing nearby held their breath to see what would happen. "Go," Jesus said. "Your faith has healed you."

Immediately, Bartimaeus opened his eyes. For the very first time, he could see the sun, big and round and yellow, as it shone on the streets of Jericho. For the very first time, Bartimaeus could see the trees nodding in the wind, and the birds perched high on their branches. Bartimaeus jumped for joy. He could see! Jesus had answered his prayer, just like Bartimaeus knew he would. Now what do you think Bartimaeus did next? He snatched up his coat and set off running down the road—and can you guess which way he went? He followed Jesus.

Think Long

What a wonderful story. How amazing that Bartimaeus was healed that very moment. Now don't you wish that all *your* prayers could be answered immediately? What do you do when God doesn't answer straight away? You wait. And even though it's hard, be patient, and *think long*. Just because your prayer isn't answered immediately, it doesn't mean that God will never answer it. Have you ever heard of a message in a bottle? It's a secret note that someone writes, seals in a bottle, and puts in the ocean, where it's carried along by the waves. The person who wrote it never knows where their message is going to end up, or who might open it. But prayers are not like that. When you pray, you can be sure where your prayer will go. You know who will open it. Your prayer is going to make its way to God, and one day, when the time is right, God will unseal your prayer and answer it—somewhere, somehow, sometime. So trust God to answer your prayer—wait, be patient, think long.

Dear God,
If my prayers aren't answered immediately, help me to be patient.
Help me to wait, and trust that you will answer my prayers
in your own time, and in your own way.
Amen.

Lord, I wait for you to help me.
Lord my God, I know you will answer.

PSALM 38:15

In the Storm

MATTHEW 8:23–27

In the middle of the Sea of Galilee, a little fishing boat dipped up and down on the waves. The boat bobbed and bounced on the water, but all that rocking didn't bother Jesus. He was tired out, curled up in a corner, his head on a comfy cushion. Jesus was taking a well-earned nap. But the disciples who were in the little boat too were getting worried. They knew this lake because they'd fished on it every day; and if those winds started to get stronger, and those waves started to get bigger, they knew they would soon be in terrible trouble. If a storm was on its way, then the last place they wanted to be was in the middle of the lake.

The disciples grabbed the oars and started rowing back to shore, but they knew it was too late as huge gray clouds came rolling in and thunder boomed above their heads. The wind picked up the waves and threw them over the deck as lightning split the sky. The disciples clung to each other as the mighty waves threatened to drag them overboard. And through it all, Jesus was still fast asleep. "Jesus! Jesus!" the terrified disciples cried. "Save us! We're going to drown."

Jesus woke up. "Where is your faith?" he asked. "Why are you so afraid?" And calmly, he stood up in the little fishing boat, held his hand out over the raging waters, and said two little words: "Be still." Immediately, just as if they recognized his voice, the wind and waves obeyed. The water was still. The thunder was silent. The wind was hushed. The storm was gone. The disciples sat down in shock. What kind of man was this, in command of wind and waves and water? Who else could say two tiny words and create one big miracle? The disciples shook their heads in wonder as they rowed back to shore on the calm, still waters of the Sea of Galilee.

God Never Sleeps

Wow! How scary for those disciples to be in the middle of a storm on the lake. No wonder they woke Jesus for help. If you are ever in a scary situation, you can cry out to God—but you'll never have to wake him up. The creator of the universe never sleeps. He is *always* watching over you. And so whenever you pray, no matter what time of day or night, you can be sure that God is always awake and always listening. How wonderful is that!

Dear God,
Thank you for always being awake,
so that you can hear every prayer.
Amen.

He who watches over you won't get tired.
In fact, he ... won't get tired or go to sleep.

PSALM 121:3–4

At the Door

LUKE 18:1–8

It was a warm day in Galilee. The disciples sat on the grassy green slopes above the lake, listening to their teacher. Jesus was doing one of the things he did best—he was telling a story.

In a certain town there lived a judge who didn't care about God, and he didn't care about people. The only person he really cared about was himself. Now in that same town there lived a widow, a poor lady whose husband had died. And as if that wasn't bad enough, someone was treating her badly.

I know, thought the poor widow to herself one day. *I'll go to the judge. I'll tell him how badly I'm being treated. He will surely listen to me and help me.* So the widow went to see the judge and knocked on the door. "Please, sir," the woman begged. "I'm being treated very badly. Can you make things right for me?" But the judge didn't have time to listen to the woman's complaints.

"Go away," he shouted rudely, and slammed the door in her face.

But the very next morning, before
the sun came up, the woman was
back, knocking on the judge's door
again. This time, the judge didn't
even open the door, even though the
woman kept knocking and knocking
until her knuckles were sore. He just
plugged his ears and went about his
business as usual. *If I ignore her*, the
judge thought to himself, *she will soon
give up*.

But the widow would *not* give up. Every single morning she would come to the judge's house, knock loudly on his door, peek through the windows, and walk circles around that house, just like Joshua walked circles around Jericho. And every day, she would plead with the judge to help her. That poor widow cried out day and night until her voice was hoarse. She pleaded with him until her tears ran dry. She circled his house until her ankles ached. She simply would *not* take no for an answer. Until finally, one day, the judge gave in. "Very well!" the judge cried. "I will make things right for you. Just stop bothering me!"

"Now," Jesus said to his disciples, "if that one unfair judge listened to that widow, how much more will your loving God listen to you? Pray hard and never give up, no matter how long it takes God to answer—because one day, you can be sure that he will."

Pray Hard

Have you ever felt like God isn't listening to your prayers? You must believe that he is! God will never shut the door on you. God will never turn his back on you. So never stop praying. Be like that widow— pray hard! Keep on circling those promises, keep on praying those prayers, and never, ever give up.

Dear God,
Help me to be like that widow in the story Jesus told.
Help me to pray, pray, pray, and never give up.
Amen.

Never stop praying.

1 THESSALONIANS 5:17

In the Quiet

It was quiet in the upper room. Oil lamps flickered and shadows grew on the wall behind the table. Jesus and his disciples had just finished a wonderful supper together. They had eaten bread and shared wine. But it had not really been a joyful time. "Every time you break bread or drink wine, think about my body being broken for you," Jesus had whispered quietly.

The disciples were confused. What did that mean? Where was Jesus going, and how would his body be broken? They huddled together in silence as Jesus knelt on the floor in the lamplight. His eyes were closed, his head was bowed. Jesus was doing what he did all the time. He was praying to his Father.

"Dear God," Jesus said. "The time has come. I've helped all people to know you, the only true God. I've brought the message of everlasting life to the world. I've finished all the work you gave me to do."

Jesus turned to look at his disciples, and then began to pray again. "Father, you see these good men you gave me? They have obeyed your word. They believe that you sent me.

I'm leaving them now, and I'm coming to you. But I'm praying for them. Be with them while they are in the world. Keep them safe so they may be one family together."

Jesus took a deep breath and paused as the lamp flames flickered again on the walls of the upper room. Then he softly began the last part of his prayer.

"Father, I pray not just for these disciples, but for everyone in the whole world who will believe in me because of their message. Let everyone who hears their words know that you sent me, and may the whole world be joined together perfectly as one wonderful family. Amen."

It was dark outside now; the time had come to leave the upper room. Jesus would never share supper with his disciples again. He knew he would soon be taken away and nailed to a cross. But he was ready. Jesus stood up and walked out into the moonlight.

Jesus Prays for You!

Did you know that on that quiet night when Jesus prayed for everyone in the whole world, he was praying for *you* too? The Bible tells us that Jesus is sitting at the right hand of his Father in heaven, where he prays for *you*. Close your eyes and try to hear that lullaby, that prayer song that Jesus is singing over you. It's a prayer that began long before you woke this morning, and will last long after you go to bed tonight. It's a prayer that started before you were born, and will continue every single day of your whole life. Can you hear it? Jesus is praying for *you*.

Dear God,
How wonderful to know that Jesus is praying for me.
Help me to think about that when I wake up in the morning,
and when I go to bed at night.
Amen.

Christ Jesus is at the right hand of God
and is also praying for us.

ROMANS 8:34

At the Tomb

JOHN 20

A breeze rustled through the trees as Mary Magdalene tiptoed into the garden. It was early in the morning. The world was still in darkness, and Mary's heart was heavy. How had that terrible thing happened? How could it be that Jesus, whose words were filled with kindness and love, was dead? Mary didn't want to believe it, but she knew it was true. She had seen him die on that cruel cross only three days earlier. She had watched as they took his body down, wrapped him in strips of linen, and carried him to this quiet cave on the hillside. Mary had run home and cried and cried. She had felt sad, alone, and helpless. But this morning when she woke, Mary realized there *was* something she could do—she could bring spices to put on Jesus' body.

Mary made her way toward the cave, but suddenly she stopped. The huge stone that had covered the entrance was gone. Mary's heart sank. This could only mean one thing—someone had stolen Jesus' body. Mary turned and fled from the cave—she had to tell the disciples.

When Peter and John heard the news, they ran without stopping until they reached the tomb, and saw for themselves the strips of linen lying quietly inside. What had happened here? Where was Jesus? None of them could understand it.

When the disciples had gone home, Mary fell to her knees and sobbed.

"Why are you crying?" a voice said behind her.

"They have taken Jesus away!" Mary cried. "Are you the gardener? Do you know where they took him?"

"Mary," the man whispered. As Mary heard her name, it seemed as if the morning darkness was suddenly gone, and the warm sun was shining on her. Mary turned toward the man. This was not the gardener! This was Jesus!

"Teacher!" she cried through her tears, as the whole world came to life around her. Flowers danced at her feet, birds sang in the trees, butterflies flew in the air, and Mary laughed out loud. Her Lord was alive! It was the most unbelievable, amazing, wonderful news anyone could ever wish to hear—and Mary couldn't wait to share it.

Just Trust

Can you imagine how Mary felt that morning? Her heart must have been singing! But how do you think she felt a few days earlier, when Jesus was arrested and taken to jail? Don't you think she must have prayed and prayed for Jesus to be set free? But if that was Mary's prayer, God's answer was *no*, because instead of Jesus being freed from jail, God had a far more wonderful plan for him. What could be more amazing than Jesus being raised from the dead? So what do you do when you pray, and the answer is no? Remember Mary. Remember that God's plans are good, and God knows best, even when you might not understand what's happening. Just trust.

Dear God,
When I pray and the answer is *no*,
help me to remember that your plans are always good,
and that you always know best.
Help me to trust.
Amen.

Trust in the Lord with all your heart.
Do not depend on your own understanding.

PROVERBS 3:5

In the Upper Room

ACTS 1:14–2:47

It was early morning when Peter woke. Just like any other morning, he climbed out of bed, ate breakfast, and set off through the narrow streets of Jerusalem toward the upper room. As he walked, Peter was thinking about Jesus. The last time he'd seen him, many weeks ago, Jesus was being carried up to heaven in the clouds. But before he left, Jesus had given the disciples a wonderful promise. "Stay in the city," Jesus told them, "and wait for the gift my Father will give." And so that's what Peter had been doing—waiting, along with all the other disciples. Just like any other ordinary day, Peter climbed the stairs to the upper room to wait some more. He didn't know it then, but as he knocked on the door and stepped inside, his day was about to become anything but ordinary—Peter was about to have the biggest holy surprise of his life.

It was quiet and dark in the upper room. The disciples greeted
each other and then bowed their heads to pray, just like they did
every morning. Suddenly, the stillness was shattered as a loud sound
came from heaven. Like the rushing of a mighty wind, it whooshed
through the windows and doors and filled every corner of the room.

The disciples cried out in surprise as tongues of fire reached out and touched each one of them. But they were not burned. Instead, the disciples jumped up, opened their mouths, and were amazed to discover they could each talk in a different language! This was the wonderful gift they had been waiting for—the disciples were filled with the Holy Spirit!

The sound of their excited voices carried through the windows and out into the streets below, where a huge crowd gathered to see what was happening. The people who had traveled to Jerusalem from many different countries stared in amazement as they heard the disciples speaking in different languages. "What's happening here?" they shouted. Peter stood on the steps of the upper room and raised his voice, with a boldness to preach that he had never felt before. "Men of Israel," Peter cried above the noise of the crowd. "We are filled with God's Holy Spirit! Listen to this! You know God sent his Son, Jesus, who did miracles and signs and wonders among us. You know Jesus was crucified, died, and was buried. After three days, God raised his Son to life, so that all of us might be saved!"

A hush fell on the crowd as they listened to Peter's words. "What shall we do?" they cried.

"Call out to Jesus," Peter said. "Ask for forgiveness for everything you've done wrong. And you will be saved. You will be filled with the Holy Spirit too. It's a promise for you, your children, and for everyone who will turn to the Lord."

And they did. Three thousand people fell to their knees that day and were baptized.

Peter knew this was just the beginning. After that day, the wonderful message of God's love for everyone and the story of Jesus' power to save would spread throughout the whole world. A day that had begun so ordinarily had turned out to be the most extraordinary day of Peter's life.

▼

Expect God's Holy Surprises!

When Peter climbed out of bed the morning of Pentecost, do you think he had any idea what would happen that day? Surely he never imagined that the Holy Spirit would come down like tongues of fire, or that he would be able to speak in a foreign language, or that three thousand people would come to know Jesus! But that's what can happen when the Holy Spirit is at work. Did you know that the gift of the Holy Spirit is a gift for you too? As you pray, remember that God's invisible Holy Spirit will be at work in your life in amazing ways. And that means that anything can happen— anytime, anyplace. Watch out for God's holy surprises!

Thank you, God,
that the gift of your Holy Spirit,
given to the disciples so long ago, is also a gift for me.
Help me to remember that even though
your Holy Spirit is invisible, he is at work in my life,
just waiting to surprise me in wonderful ways.
Amen.

You will receive the gift of the Holy Spirit.

ACTS 2:38

In the City

ACTS 9:1–20

Saul had a goal in mind, and nothing would stop him. He pounded his fist fiercely on the table and shouted in a loud voice, "Let me go to Damascus—today! I'll show those believers who's in charge. I'll stop them from spreading their lies about Jesus! He was *not* God's Son, and he didn't come back to life. I'll throw all those believers in jail!"

The high priest nodded his head. "Very well, Saul," he replied. "Go." Saul saddled up his horse, gathered his men, and set off at a gallop. Dust flew high in the air as the horses' hooves pounded the

road to Damascus. But suddenly the biggest, brightest, most dazzling light Saul had ever seen split the skies open and flashed around them. The horses reared up in fear, and Saul fell to the ground as a voice came from heaven. "Saul, Saul, why are you fighting me?"

"Who are you, Lord?" Saul cried.

"I am Jesus, the one you are fighting against. Now get up, go into the city, and there you will be told what to do."

This was unbelievable news to Saul. He staggered to his feet
and found, to his horror, that he was blind. He groped around in
darkness until he felt the hand of one of his men. "Take me into the
city," he said. "I cannot see."

In a little house in Damascus, Saul fell to his knees and prayed
like he had never prayed before. He knew now that everything he
had ever heard about Jesus must be true. How very wrong he'd been
to try to imprison all the believers. For three days, Saul lived in total
darkness. Until one morning, when Ananias knocked on the door.

"Brother Saul," Ananias said quietly. "The Lord Jesus, who appeared to you on the road, has sent me to you, so that you might see again and be filled with the Holy Spirit." At the touch of this man's hand, Saul opened his eyes and was overjoyed to find that he could see again. He jumped up, got baptized, and went straight out into the streets and synagogues of the city, ready to preach the good news about Jesus to everyone who would listen.

Saul had a new goal now. He was a changed man. Saul, who had hated Jesus, became Paul, who loved Jesus. He spent the rest of his life traveling all over the world, encouraging others, writing letters to churches, preaching, and praying for believers everywhere. And even though he was shipwrecked, thrown in prison for his faith, beaten, starved, and laughed at, Paul never lost sight of his goal—to tell the whole world the wonderful truth about Jesus.

Let Your Goals Be God's Goals

Did you notice how Paul changed his goals in life after he came to know Jesus? Paul decided to let his goals be God's goals. He chose to use the gifts and talents God gave him to make a difference in the world. Did you know that even though Paul died 2,000 years ago, he is still achieving the goals he set for himself? The Bible contains the letters that Paul wrote to the churches all those years ago, and so his words are *still* bringing people to Jesus. Something powerful happens when our goals in life are God's goals for us too. Do you think you're too young to have goals for your life? You're not! As you pray, ask God to show you what his goals for your life might be, and then ask him to help you achieve them. Together, you'll make a great team—and you'll be able to make a difference in the world too.

Dear God,
Please show me what your goals for my life might be.
Help me to discover the gifts and talents you've given me,
so that I'll be able to use them in the way you want me to.
Amen.

I push myself forward toward the goal to win the prize …
The heavenly prize is Christ Jesus himself.

PHILIPPIANS 3:14

By the River

ACTS 16:11–15

Lydia folded the last piece of purple cloth and laid it carefully beside her chair. It was expensive. She would sell it at the market tomorrow, but right now, she had more important business to attend to. She needed to pray.

Lydia closed the door to her home and walked down to the river, where she knew her friends would be waiting. This was a beautiful place to pray together. The sound of the water running by as it trickled over the stones, and the sight of the willow trees hanging over the bank always helped Lydia feel close to God. It was, after all, his creation.

Lydia and her friends bowed their heads and whispered their prayers into the wind.

"May we join you?" a man's voice said. Lydia looked up to see Paul and his companions.

"Of course," she replied. "All are welcome to pray here."

Lydia listened carefully as Paul—who had traveled all the way from Israel, over land and sea—began to preach. He talked about a wonderful man called Jesus, who was God's own Son. Jesus had made the blind see, taught people how to love, and had miraculously come back to life three days after he'd died. And as she listened to Paul's words, Lydia felt a stirring in her heart, just as if Jesus were whispering her name. "I want to know Jesus!" Lydia cried.

"Then it's simple," Paul said. "Let me baptize you, and Jesus will be by your side forever."

That very day, Lydia and all the members of her household were baptized in the cleansing waters of the river, and after that, whenever Paul and his companions traveled to Philippi, they stayed at Lydia's home. And every day, whenever Lydia went to the river to pray, she remembered the wonderful day she was baptized, the wonderful day she came to know Jesus.

Prayer Brings Us Closer to God

Do you have a special place to pray, like Lydia did? Is there somewhere you feel especially close to God? Wherever you pray, you must know one wonderful thing—your prayers never, ever die. They live forever. Those prayers that Lydia whispered over the river? They were carried to heaven, where they echo in eternity. Those prayers you said yesterday? They are not gone. They last forever. Those prayers your parents and grandparents prayed for you before you were even born? They last and last through generations, bringing us closer and closer to God—how wonderful is that!

Dear God,
Thank you so much that when I pray,
it brings me closer and closer to you.
How amazing to think that my prayers are never lost, or gone.
And even though it's hard for me to understand,
thank you that my prayers never die, but last forever.
Amen.

Come near to God,
and he will come near to you.

JAMES 4:8

In the Jail

ACTS 16:22–35

From deep in the prison came the sweet sound of singing.
It echoed up through the cold, damp, dark jail, traveled along the
corridors, and crept through the keyholes of every cell. All the
prisoners who heard that sweet sound were amazed. They lay on
their mats, listening in wonder. This was not the sound they were
used to hearing. That cold, dark, damp jail was usually full of the
sounds of crying, screaming, wailing, and moaning. But not tonight.
Tonight was different. Paul and Silas, those two men who believed
in Jesus and would not stop talking about him, were singing prayers
and praises to God at the tops of their voices. How could they do
that when they were in such a horrible place? They had already
been stripped, beaten, and tortured. They'd been carried down
to the deepest part of the jail and thrown into the dungeon. But
instead of being filled with self-pity, they were filled with peace!
It did not make sense.

The miracle happened at the stroke of midnight. A violent earthquake struck the jail. It shook every floor and every room. Every iron door flew open and every heavy chain fell off. The prisoners were free! The jailer who was guarding Paul and Silas knew he was in big trouble. He took out his sword, ready to take his own life, but Paul cried out, "No, no! Don't do that! We won't run away. We're right here."

"Turn the lights on!" the jailer cried as he ran to see what had happened. Shaking from head to toe, the jailer fell to his knees in front of Paul and Silas. "Tell me what I need to do to be saved," he said.

"Believe in the Lord Jesus," Paul said quietly. "Then you and all your family will be saved."

The jailer did not waste a minute. He took Paul and Silas to his home and gently washed their wounds. And even though it was still the middle of the night, the jailer, his family, and all who lived in his house were baptized.

Later, Paul and Silas sat with everyone at the jailer's table. They shared a lovely meal together, talked about Jesus, and told the amazing story of what had happened that night. The whole room, and everyone's hearts, were filled with joy.

Praise God No Matter What!

It's hard to imagine anything worse than being beaten and thrown into a dark jail. But even in that terrible situation, Paul and Silas chose to pray and sing. And do you know what happened? Instead of being filled with fear, Paul and Silas were filled with peace. Life can be full of challenges; things might go wrong, and sometimes bad things happen. But God is with us through it all, waiting to hold our hand through every storm—waiting to bring us his peace. And if you can manage to praise God, even in hard times, God's wonderful peace will be yours.

Dear God,
Thank you that whatever I might go through, you are always there, holding out your hand to me, ready to give me your peace.
Help me to praise you, no matter what.
Amen.

Don't worry about anything. No matter what happens,
tell God about everything. Ask and pray, and give thanks to him.
Then God's peace will watch over your hearts and your minds.

PHILIPPIANS 4:6–7

On the Island

REVELATION 3:7–8; 5:11–13; 21

John was a very old man. He closed his eyes and thought about all that had happened in his life. He remembered that day, long ago, when Jesus called him and his brother as they were mending their fishing nets on the shore. He remembered all the wonderful times he'd spent with Jesus, and all the amazing miracles he'd seen.

He would never forget how Jesus fed five thousand hungry people with one small lunch, how he'd calmed the storm to a whisper, and how he healed blind Bartimaeus without even touching him. He remembered that awful night when Jesus was taken away and crucified, and how, three days later, he'd come back to life. How amazing that had been! But all that was long ago now. John was all alone, sent far away to this island because of his faith.

John closed his eyes. Was he dreaming now? Was that an angel he could *see*? And whose voice was that, sounding like a trumpet behind him?

"John," said the voice. "Don't be afraid. I am the First and the Last, the Beginning and the End, the one who was dead—but now I am alive for ever and ever. Write down everything you see."

John stared in amazement as a door opened in front of him. It was the very door to heaven. And there, on the throne, sat one who sparkled like jewels, surrounded by a rainbow and a shimmering sea of glass. As John watched, thousands and thousands of angels flew around the throne, singing with every creature in heaven and on earth:

To him who sits upon the throne, give honor, praise, and might.

To him who sits upon the throne, sing glory day and night.

"I am making everything new, John!" cried the one who sat upon the throne. "And in this wonderful new place, God will come to live with his people. There'll be no more crying, and no more sadness, and no more pain." John could hardly believe his eyes as he saw a glorious new heaven, where the shining streets were made of gold and the walls glittered with jewels. The gates of heaven were open wide for all God's people to come inside, and there was no night or darkness there because God's brilliant light poured in and filled every single space.

"Behold, I'm coming soon, John," said the voice of Jesus.

wonderful things he'd seen and heard. And the very last word that John wrote is the word we say at the end of all our prayers:
Amen.

Where Our Prayers End, God Begins

Do you know what "amen" means? It means "let it be so"' or "it is true." We use amen to end our prayers, but guess what? The end of a prayer is always just the beginning. It's the beginning of a dream. It's the beginning of a miracle. It's the beginning of a promise. Where our prayers end, God begins! When God hears our prayers, whether we say them out loud or in our heads; whether we're in church or at home; whether we're kneeling or standing, God begins his wonderful work in our lives and in the world. The one who hovered over creation at the beginning of all time is hovering over your life too—waiting to hear and answer your prayers. So remember to pray hard, circle your dreams, never give up, and above all, remember that our great God is with you, watching over you, keeping his promises, and listening to every cry of your heart. Amen.

Awesome God,
Thank you for this book I hold. Thank you for this life I live.
Thank you for the wonderful knowledge that you are right here
beside me as I pray. Lead me every day, closer and closer to you.
And every plan and purpose you have for my life, let it be so.
Amen

God began a good work in you. And I am sure
that he will carry it on until it is completed.
That will be on the day Christ Jesus returns.

PHILIPPIANS 1:6

More to Love
from Mark Batterson

FOR KIDS & STUDENTS

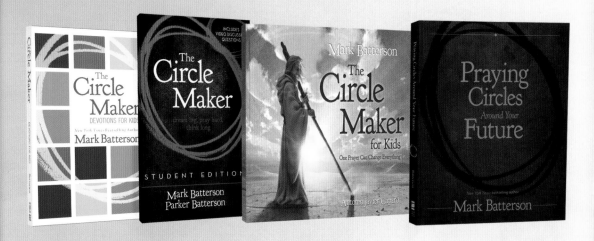

The Circle Maker	The Circle Maker	The Circle Maker	Praying Circles Around
Devotions for Kids	Student Edition	for Kids	Your Future
978-0-310-76681-0	978-0-310-75036-9	978-0-310-72492-6	978-0-310-76615-5

and The Circle Maker brand

FOR PARENTS

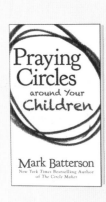
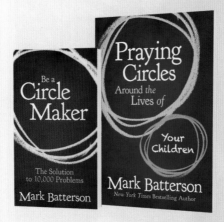

Praying Circles Around Your Children
978-0-310-32550-5

Be A Circle Maker: The Solution to 10,000 Problems
978-0-310-33635-8

Praying Circles Around the Lives of Your Children
978-0-310-33973-1

The Circle Maker
978-0-310-34691-3

Available wherever books are sold!